DEDICATION

Clark Bancroft Perry (1947-2011)
Frederick Gardiner Perry
Sheldon Pettibone Perry and Nina Sawicki Perry
Steven Crosby Perry (1953-2018)

≈

Susan Irene Swanton
Carolyn Lois Swanton

≈

Ross Bertam Capon and Louise Inman Capon

≈

George David Waldman and Mallory Clark Waldman
Thomas Bernham Scheffey and Melissa Clark Scheffey
Jennifer Clark
Charles Stevens and Alison Clark Stevens

ENDORSEMENT

I thoroughly enjoyed reading each poem in *Water Voices*, and found them, overall, to be a beautiful, thoughtful exploration of spirituality as it is reflected and reaffirmed by our experiences with nature. I particularly enjoyed how this collection was structured as a journey – from Calm to Storm to Peace, but also from the innocent, carelessness of childhood to acceptance of the harsher realities of adulthood, the so-called 'real' world. What a unique and personal take on a bildungsroman and the journey of transition throughout our ages. I am sure that many will see themselves in Sheldon Clark's work, which might provoke them to think more deeply.

Cinde Lock, Ph. D.
Queen's University, 2002
Head of School, Pickering College, Newmarket, Ontario

≈≈≈

I read *Water Voices* in one sitting. I delighted in the joys, dreams, and innocent experiences of childhood. I ventured into the second section of the challenges presented in "Storm." The moving current of the narratives carried me with their undertow into dark depths. Some "cumulous heights" of positive change and gratitude are illuminated in the third section. Sheldon grounds his experience clearly motivated by scripture. My favorite poem is "Unspoken Depths" because it so beautifully captures the excitement and movement of the Divine Spirit at work in a Quaker Meeting. Sheldon's reflective descriptions continue to speak to me. They are refreshing and encouraging. I am challenged to listen more attentively to the "water voices" that speak in subtle and stirring ways.

Virginia Walsh, M.A. (English)
York University, Toronto, Ontario, 1979

I do appreciate Sheldon Clark's reflections on the spiritual inspiration of his early life. I identify with the deepening significance of those early and growing influences that impacted his spiritual development and his ability to bring them more clearly and poignantly into his present experience. From our common Quaker connection, Clark articulates the flowing and ripening awareness of personal and social understanding, enabling us to grow as brethren in the spirit. We share a Quaker understanding of connection, of overcoming the flux of time and the blocks thrown in our way by a world of intolerance and conflict. Water Voices remind us of our unity as human beings in the flow of time, resisting the undercurrents that too often make us forget our common origin and our search for Truth. We live in a world of confusing diversions that draw us further and further apart. Clark's water imagery reminds me to be more attentive to the water voices that continually inspire us to share developments in our spiritual journeys.

Keith R. Maddock, M. Th.
Toronto School of Theology, Emmanuel College, University of Toronto, 1994

ACKNOWLEDGEMENTS

Water Voices are narrative records of memories, happenings, contemplative worship, current events, reflective reading, and several significant educational events. Encouragement came from past and present friends including Harry M. Beer (1913-1987), Christina Brookes, Thomas S. Brown III (1912-2011), Annette Colenbrader, Melissa Grimaldi, Ruth Hannay, J. Bernard Haviland (1915-2004), Rev. Holly Hoffman, V. Ishvarmurti, Barbara Brown MacDonald, Denise McKay, Amber McPhail, Ryan McPhail, Rev. Dr. F. Gardiner Perry, Sheldon Pettibone Perry, Marvin H. Shagam (1924-2016), R. Fox Smith (1911-1975), Dorothy Virginia Walsh, and Arlene Wassink.

Sheldon H. Clark
2023

≈≈

PREVIOUS PUBLICATIONS

Fire Voices, by Sheldon H. Clark with Amber C. McPhail, 2022
After the Fire A Still Small Voice, by Sheldon H. Clark with Catherine Farquhar, 2022
Still Voices, by Sheldon H. Clark, 2020, 2021
Voices Extended, by Neil Paul and Sheldon H. Clark, 2016
Poetry and Prayer Sketches, by Sheldon H. Clark with George S. Keltika, 2013

Published by Rock's Mills Press, Oakville, Ontario, Canada
www.rocksmillspress.com
For information, please contact us at customer.service@rocksmillspress.com

Copyright © 2023, by Sheldon H. Clark
All rights reserved

(All imagery sourced from Public Domain or by Amber C. McPhail)

PREFACE

The earth is the Lord's, and the fulness thereof;
The world, and they that dwell therein.
For he hath founded it upon the seas,
And established it upon the floods.
                                    Psalm 24:1-2

    In the summer of 1958, my brother and I rode horseback into the hill ring surrounding a cattle ranch near Gunnison, Colorado. We followed a creek to its spring, dismounted, and we and our horses refreshed ourselves with cool clear water. We felt history flowing down our throats. We felt at one with the eternal source sending cleansing blood through our veins. We gave thanks for this natural baptism. I could only wish that people everywhere could give thanks for the unmerited gift of pure water.

    Water voices are heard in varieties of music from classical, gospel, country and western, folk, easy listening, and rock. Water voices are seen in drawings, paintings, and photography, as representative, abstract, and mood inspiring. Water voices in literature appeal to the five senses and express inner thoughts. Words are the instruments used to articulate passionate love, reflect on grief, loss, danger, and death, and are intentionally chosen to provoke a response.

    Water voices are as constant as sunrise and sunset. They possess character. They are as soothing as divine mercy. They are as gentle as the lion that lies down with the lamb, as violent as unbridled war and storms at sea, as miraculous as spiritual conversion, as nourishing as Mother Earth, and as mysterious as love. In listening to water voices, we hear the divine replenishing Creation, itself.

    The narrative poems in Water Voices were inspired to acknowledge each person's experience as they bring their welcoming capabilities to our essential source of existence. In these uncertain times of climate change, it is incumbent upon humanity to listen to water voices as friendly sounds ever so subtly appealing for human help to achieve the goals of balance, conservation, restorative justice, and mutually assured survival.

                                                                Sheldon

God My Constant Companion and Source of Inner Strength

God, my constant companion, and source of inner strength,
Thank you, for Your many blessings.
Let my life be guided by Your Love.
May I have the strength, wisdom, and courage
to respond to the promptings of the Light within.
May I be sensitive, understanding, and compassionate
in my relations with others.
May I seek and find that which is good,
true, beautiful, and joyous.
May I seek the truth, so that Your Will may be done.
Amen.

Dorothy Trimble (1923-2014)
Yonge Street Friends Meeting, Newmarket, Ontario
Used with permission of the Dorothy Trimble Estate

CONTENTS

Dedication
Endorsement
Acknowledgements
Preface
Prayer by Dorothy
Contents

CALM

Opening Prayer
Birth
Glimmerings
Water Gifts
Unspoken Depths

STORM

Who Bear Best His Mild Yoke, They Serve Him Best
Ukraine's Hope
What Happened to Time?
Dislocation
Sacrifice, A Short Story

PEACE

Metanoia
The Dance Rhythm
Trust Charles, A Short Story
Health
The Question is Not One of Mercy's Gifts
Closing Prayer

CALM

OPENING PRAYER

Let the words of my mouth,
And the meditation of my heart, be acceptable in thy sight,
O Lord, my strength, and my redeemer.

Psalm 19:14

Divine Creator,
the cosmos, the planets, the seen
and the unseen are Yours.
Creation is Yours.

You brought Light out of Darkness.
You gathered Your children
to tend moors and mountains,
fields and streams,
lakes and oceans,
lands and airwaves that
disappear into the infinite blue.

We pray for Your guidance,
to hear and heed
Your sweet compassionate orchestration.
Let us arise from the ashes of pride
and bear witness to Your Divine Glory.

Amen.

BIRTH

For it was you who formed my inward parts;
you knit me together in my mother's womb.

Psalm 139:13 **(NRSV)**

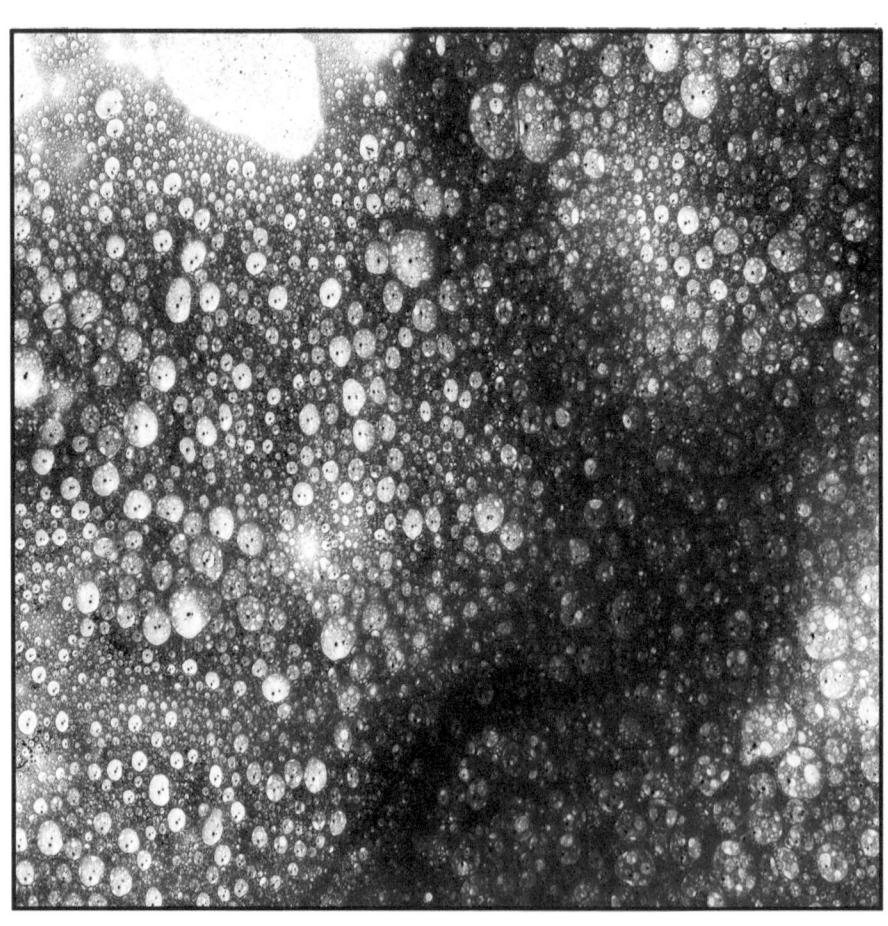

Birth from darkness is joy-filled as the amniotic fluid prepares the way
from post-partum to connected bonding from life-giving to light-receiving.
Newborns thrive on caressing, nurturing, eliminating, exerting,
sleeping, as instinctive patterns form, as sure as foals follow their dams.
Mother and child sculpt their symbiotic relationship while
she nourishes and the young suckles inhabiting the splendor of being and becoming.
Milk production is reciprocal.
Nourishment for health and growth and for transformational certainty
merge into a syncopated dance.

≈≈≈≈≈

The counselor, eighteen years old, was taught to revere life,
trained in Red Cross first aid and life-saving,
took charge of the six-year-old campers for
a much-anticipated shorts-only creek hike.
This July afternoon was humid. The sun produced
upward-bound pale steam beams from dying grasses.
The creek walk capped the journey from the pungent
mossy escarpment through the field to the brook.
T-shirts and sneakers were flung off willy-nilly.
Safety-first! The whistle means, silence, line up.

READY. STEADY. GO!

Run. Jump. Splash. Submerge. Arise. Breathe.
Screams made the minnows dash downstream for safety.
Then it happened. "Help." Whistle. "Rangers!"
The counselor waded, reached, lifted, carried, and
slapped the child's back. Tear breaths signaled mercifully
as though the newborn had caught their first breath. They stood
silently in awe as life's breath changed darkness into light.

GLIMMERINGS
Fairmount Nursery, 1945

Miss Adelaide knew my name.
She had a melodious way of roll calling.
My insides knew she cared.
My heart's new feelings were mysterious.
My mother and Ms. Adelaide knew.
She became my lovely big sister.

We pumped the swing with our short legs.
Held the rope as high as we could reach.
Run forward. Time the seat swing.
Jump. Sit. Lean back. Pull. Pump.
Higher. Faster. Slower.
Repeat. Run. Jump. Pump. Repeat.

I loved swinging and sunbursts of sheer joy.
I loved the jungle gym twisting.
I loved hanging like a monkey.
I loved getting lost in the jungle bars.
I loved emerging.
I loved upside down, sideways, towhead-side up.

From top bars, I saw a garden over the fence.
Tall trees. Habit-clad nuns prayed along cedar chip paths.
Daisies, daffodils, lavender, cowslip, bluebells,
Fescue grasses and fecund soil listened to inner prayers.
Our rambunctious class listened silently at Storytime.
Fathers' cast-off shirts were transformed into art smocks.

Ms. Adelaide waited each noon. She held my hand.
Our mother could tell I was happy.
I loved Miss Adelaide.
She was beautiful.
I liked sitting near her.
Miss Adelaide cared.

WATER GIFT

*I know that there is nothing better for them than
to be happy and enjoy themselves as long as they live.*
							Ecclesiastes 3:12a **(NRSV)**

Swimming lessons mean fun, discovery, trust.
Young Olympians enjoy individual attention.
Safety, comfort, and security are enhanced by a shallow pool.
A warm sun, a blue-sky day, and fluffy clouds
create confidence as tyros explore becoming adept.
Trust evolves.

Swimming is like drifting into a dream.
Four never-before swimmers and personal instructors
enter the crystal blue water.
The reassuring voice floated in the air,
Let's get wet all over, dip down, and stand up.
Let's turn around, dip and stand and shake all over like a puppy.

Left ear. Right ear. Deep breath. Hold. Release.
Bend forward. Deep breath. Release. Repeat.
Deep breath. Stand. Breathe. Release and repeat.
Now, make an arc from ear to ear in the water.
Left ear. Right ear. Up.
Breathe. Hold. Release. Relax.

Today is dead-man-float. Face Bill, Nancy, Doug, and Barbara.
Imitate. Stand tall. Hands overhead. Become a human arrow.
Bend the knees. Bend at the waist. Deep breath.
Push into the glide along the wrinkled glass surface.
Float forward to your swimming friend.
Stand. Breathe. Relax.

Coast back and forth like a frog gliding in a lily pond.
Coast to your in-water buddies.
Kick like a frog. Quick together. Glide.
Again. Frog kick. Smooth, slow glide. Reach out.
Back and forth, back and forth, back and forth.
Heads up and pull yourself through the water.

Tadpoles become frogs. Tiny increments lead to competence.
Dreams are buoyant reminders of future possibilities.
Visions lead to confident floating, treading, rhythmic coordination
of body, hands, legs, breathing, speed, turning,
ballet-like movement, water polo, racing, and diving.

Swim from the shallows into the deep.
Dismiss fear of the impossible by trial and achievement.
Live for the dream.
Love art for art's sake.
Jump like a transcendent dolphin above the spume
for the sheer joy of living.
Love success as you join your dreams.

UNSPOKEN DEPTHS

God is a Spirit: and they that worship must worship him
In spirit and in truth.

John 4:24

Friends Meeting
occasions unspoken depths.
Oceanic deep-down darkness
wells up to surface
whitecaps
exhaled to cumulus heights.

Perceived as Storm or Light,
the thunderous rainbow spectrum
Disappears into pitch and roll
indistinguishable from
the mystery of being and becoming.

The Light, known in part,
internally, celestially,
are intuited not as sound,
but rather felt in soaring twirling funnels
as visions melt into air, into thin air.

The Light, like effervescent spume,
stirs … swirls … settles …
back to the deep
Mysterium Tremendum.

Friends Meeting
draws, lifts, releases
the diffusing Light into
enigmatic darkness.

STORM

WHO BEST BEAR HIS MILD YOKE, THEY SERVE HIM BEST

Who Best Bear His Mild Yoke, They Serve Him Best.
                          Sonnet 19, John Milton (1608-1674)

Jesus encouraged.
   - *Follow me, and I will make you fishers of men.*
   - *Blessed are the peacemakers: for they shall be called the children of God.*
   - *Ye are the salt of the earth,*
   - *Ye are the light of the world*
   - *For where your treasure is, there will your heart be also.*
   - *If any man will come after me, let him deny himself,*
     and take up his cross, and follow me.
       Fishermen wait for the weather, to cast nets, catch, and market.

Jesus motivated.
   - *As thou hast believed, so be it done unto thee.*
   - *Thy sins are forgiven.*
   - *Behold, I send you forth as sheep in the midst of wolves:*
     be ye therefore wise as serpents, and harmless as doves.
   - *Heal the sick, cleanse the lepers, raise the dead, cast out devils:*
     freely ye have received, freely give.
   - *For where two or three are gathered together in my name,*
     there am I in the midst of them.
   - *Go home to thy friends,*
     and tell them how great things the Lord hath done for thee,
     and hath had compassion on thee.
       Farmers wait for the seasons, to cultivate, harvest, and market.

Jesus told Parables.
- *The kingdom of heaven is like a grain of mustard seed.*
- *The wind bloweth where it listeth, and thou hearest the sound thereof, but canst not tell whence it cometh, and whither it goeth: so is every one that is born of the Spirit.*
- *I am the living bread which came down from heaven.*
- *I am the light of the world: he that followeth me shall not walk in darkness, but shall have the light of life.*
- *I am the door. I am the good shepherd. I am the resurrection and the life. I am the way, the truth, and the life. I am the true vine.*

    Fishermen, farmers, and just plain folks generate transformational living.

Jesus showed compassion.
- *Therefore all things whatsoever ye would that men should do to you, ye even so to them; for this is the law and the prophets.*
- *Thy faith hath made thee whole.*
- *Thy sins be forgiven thee.*
- *A good man out of the good treasure of the heart bringeth forth good things.*
- *Inasmuch as ye have done it unto one of the least of these my brethren, ye have done it unto me.*
- *Be not afraid.*

    Fishermen, farmers, and just plain folks care about people, places, things.

Jesus forgave.
- *Thou forgavest the iniquity of my sins.*
- *Let her alone; why trouble ye her? She hath wrought a good work on me.*
- *It is meet that we should make merry, and be glad: for this thy brother was dead, and is alive again; and was lost, and is found.*
- *Suffer little children to come unto me, and forbid them not: for of such is the kingdom of God.*
- *Father, forgive them; for they know not what they do.*
- *Feed my lambs. Feed my sheep. Follow me.*

Fishermen, farmers, and just plain folks love domestic tranquility.

Jesus expected.
Whosoever greets each day as though it is their first and last; encounters serenity.
Whosoever shares food, clothing, and shelter; encounters harmony.
Whosoever creates the beloved community; encounters peace.
Whosoever reaps friendship, hope, and love; encounters faith.
Whosoever earns their daily bread; encounters contentment.
Whosoever lives a life fulfilled; encounters the Creator.

They also serve who only stand and wait.

≈≈≈≈≈≈≈≈≈≈≈≈≈≈≈≈≈≈≈≈≈≈≈≈≈≈≈≈≈≈

UKRAINE'S HOPE
(*In Memorium* - Lysya Ukrainka (1871-1913))

Television flickering static images
pronounce sudden clarity
as a reporter's camera scans
scarecrow buildings, wasteland, the dead.
Absent people, body-bagged corpses
readied for pick up by determined
volunteer drivers in converted autos
ambulance their patient cargo away.
Since 1854, when Roger Fenton assigned to Crimea
photographed dismembered vacant stares, he
piqued the consciences of Victorians who skeptically saw photos
of smoke-filled air and the waterless grey skies of grief.
Propellent death hovers waiting for new wind and rain
to wipe away the perfume sting of obscene filth
from electronic eyes that record for posterity
atrocity, brutality, barbarity, cruelty, violence.
Blown-apart apartment skeletons
premature winter-like denuded trees
intentional targets of an inhumane slog
metaphorically suck clean the marrow of unsuspecting organisms.
Belligerents disfigured alike by the Martial Beast
want this rite of mutually assured annihilation to end
this atmosphere of discordant nightmares
and dissipate into nothingness.
Ukraine's peace portrait is that in which flora and fauna alike,
return as Springtime pastel entities, to be watered,
to bend, to labor with creative force,
to seed the moist forgiving ground with
winter wheat for worldwide nourishment.

WHAT HAPPENED TO TIME?
(Izyum, Ukraine: 49°12′46″N 37°15′25″E)

Hour, date, day, month, year never mind the waste.
Cat sat and watched the drip spring on the crystal leaf.
She expected a mouse to twitch to the constant drill.
Present tense, always present tense dismissed.
Future history as though with a muffled gong struck dumb.

The AK-74M is light, reliable, has low recoil and is compact with the standard issue folding plastic buttstock.

Light dark took switch-yard turns
Two times each day, dark-light, light-dark.
The mist concealed fragmented time-unheard sound.
Tick tock. Drip drop. Si-lent. Si-lent.
Cat bunched shifted a whisker maybe flickered.

The Glock is currently one of the most popular military and police sidearms worldwide, including with U.S. Army special forces and elite units in the Russian security services.

Mud? Frigid slush? Hard pack?
Brown olive green gray
Faded washed out, not in, the better
to conform
To the monotony, the camaraderie between timeless
Wasted colorless bland formless nothingness.
Cat held the drip on the leaf as a silent sentry to inaction.

While Kalashnikov's machine gun is less famous than his rifle, in many ways it is a better design. Lighter than most Western 7.62 machine guns, it is still accurate and controllable. The PKM has proven popular with almost every country that's used it.

Dress codes are long gone from razor creases.
Minds void are unresponsive to imaginative wanderings.
Forgotten are memories of what was and what will become.
The respite is the stop-start of weight shifting to be at ease.
The cat drifted tightly into a wound-up spring.

The MP5 is ubiquitous around the world in the hands of special police units, and Russia is no exception.

Deprived of caress, gaze, pong, hum-or-wail, no traces
Just wounded impotency flagged without hope
No pursuit without will without expectation
Without quaver without being, but simply being.
Cat intent, timeless, still, absorbed, aspirant.

Sako TRG rifles are the most popular with Russian elite snipers, beating out the domestic SV-98 and Orsis rifles.

Drip leaf shuddered
Fog wilted wet mist gray to scorched umber
Nanosecond trembled just once
Air separated faster than the cosmic tail of a faded star
Cat pounced, fell, and lay amidst the silt; collateral litter.

Quotations:
Gao, Charlie. *The National Interest.* June 22, 2020.
https://nationalinterest.org/blog/reboot/here-are-5-guns-russian-military-loves-163254?curator=TechREDEF

DISLOCATION

Faint grey smoke, sensed, not seen,
floated from earth's side of heaven, then
ghosted away to join the grey wet wind.
Six AM start, quick feed, turn out, muck seven horses.
The October day promised escape.
Seven-thirty. Five of seven were brought safely to fresh hay.
Two pregnant mares to go before cold rain set in.
We, too, had the promise of something old something new.
Wet mist forecast, "Hurry up."
"Haste makes waste," echoed memorialized advice.
Make efficient use of time.
Memorial worship is two-hour drive north.
Wash. Change. Be ready.
Dismembered feelings wanted patience.
The green metal gate cracked open.
The first mare out was not to be denied uncut fescue.
He took the lead left-handed while the right fist closed on the noseband.
Impossible. The other turned to secure the second mare.
The jolted shoulder dislocation matched the speed of the mare's loss and her greedy inhale of grass. The prone human considered options.
Rain fell. Gate closed against the second mare's escape.
Casually, his partner retrieved the snaked lead.
First mare, now sated, permitted the stable saunter.
Second mare anxiously danced alone.
Emergency telephoned. The fallen comforted. Retrieve the worried fenced-in mare.
Time suspended. Mist, transited to downpour, plans swerved.
Pain injection for the bumpy hospital trip.
The family gathered and saw the need, their duty, and their necessity to carry on.
His partner sustained his renewal with her soft calm voice.
A dislocated shoulder dismembered instantaneously seventy-five years of riding across fields and streams, through apple orchards, pine groves, and maple bush, always up and over, away! Imperial B. Good, Claudia, Mickey, Barney, Becket, Shayla, remembered. Thrown to sedentary convalescent, poetic urgencies.
Wry humor hinted, "Justice."

SACRIFICE

Greater love hath no man than this, that a man lay down his life for his friends.

John 15:13

Bleak hot rain swept across the wasteland, the no-man's land. Vaporous mist rose from the hard-packed clay. Reddish brown, greens, blues, and blacks blurred in the whitish grey-green mist. No bush or tree broke the monotony of the splashed landscape. The darkening misty night-falling sky served as a protective blanket over this nada land.

Cracks of thunder flashed spectral streaks across the hidden faces. Not a single person jerked in protest to the call of the elements. Men, women, and children clad in rags stifled their inklings of fear.

Cannonade from the heavens continued and the earth was blinded for a moment in bright light. Then, there was darkness. The close suffocation of sweating bodies cramped together was unable to move, not even for comfort. Children buried their faces in their mothers' laps and breasts against the noise, the dark, and their terrifying fear.

Explosion! Flame! Tightness!

Boom! Boom! Boom! Six adults and five children slipped, waded, scurried, and eliminated in continuous dread. The soft voices lowing, as cattle will, momentarily penetrating the stillness after the horrific noise and light flashes. Adults kept vigil. They waited for some sign. Snakes wormed their way across the land in search of higher ground. One of the men suddenly planted his foot on the writhing stick in front of him. "We have to leave." They filed furtively out of the shadows toward the copse. "Watch where you step." "Shh. Listen." They froze and lay down. One touched his ear to the ground. "Hunters. We have to move."

The thin line hurried as if the dark-cloaked scythe carrier was leading them. "Shh. We'll be safe in a second."

Lightning flashed lighting the nada land. The wet compost under the thicket was within reach, so close.

Lightning flashed. A hound let cry. Then, it seemed that tens, even hundreds of hounds gave tongue drowning out the thunder and the fresh downpour.

"Run down the creek. Cross over. Scurry for your lives!"

Panic. Flash flood. Flight.

Riders loomed through the steady rain. Bullwhips tore at retreating flesh. Hooves slipped and trampled over three fallen bodies. The scramble, the contact was quick and over. Lightning flashed. A hunter saw the man and then heard him yell, "Run for your lives. I'll stop this one."

Seven ran for the woods. The mounted hunter charged. "This way." The swaying hunched bush sprang and grabbed the horse's reins as it shied. Blood spurted from the horse's mouth. It whinnied and reared in protest throwing its rider.

Two men faced each other. Both looked like identical mud twins. As practiced wrestlers do, they circled each other cautiously, simultaneously lunging for the other's throat, crotch, arm, or leg to grapple as one mud ball knot. The hunter's call had brought him help. The quarry overpowered was kicked, beaten, hog-tied, and petrified.

"Boys, look what I caught. I felt like Jacob wrestling with the stranger. Now, I am going to have some fun."

The man's sarcasm choked the other.

"He sure don't say much. Maybe he don't speak. Hey, say something to me. We're your friends. Your judge and jury, too. Where ya goin' in such a hurry? Who's with you? Help us and we'll help you. Don't be afraid of nothing."

"Gimme a whip. He'll talk." The whip cut through the air.

"He don't even cry."

"Our Father, who ..t .n heaven, hallow…," he mouthed.

"What you saying?"

"Let's get him."

"Get him! Get him! Get him!" chanted the mob. Hounds lay down panting and watched.

The circle tightened like a noose on the fugitive, who lay trapped like an animal. Feet, fists, yells, and screams amidst the mud slick, pummeled the defenseless soul. Thunder and lightning sounded a fading unearthly rumble of surrender.

The knife gleamed and the scar of its sharp edge riveted the orgiastic men and their victim. The steel was viciously thrust into the man's chest.

The mob, as if touched by his passion, drew away. They stared at the contorted figure on the ground. One relieved himself.

Horses, hounds, and the satiated scared-to-death hunters evaporated.

"God."

Thunder, lightning, and then the rain stopped.

PEACE

METANOIA

__Repent: for the kingdom of heaven is at hand.__
                                                Matthew 4:17

I sought wealth and became possessive.
I sought fame and became prideful.
I sought power and became afraid.

I shared wealth and found inner peace.
I suffered sorrow and found compassion.
I became vulnerable and found love.

THE DANCE RHYTHM

How can we know the dancer from the dance?
W. B. Yeats (1865-1939)

Approach slowly
a syncopated graceful
respect for points of balance.
The dance welling from a
sensory source becomes inevitable
an ancient source
enigmatic power
rites of passage
the hunt

Control slowly
near separation
centrifugal expansion
style a quickened pace
circles expand contract
hidden pungent cascades
blessed with complimentary
sympathetic design pulsations
providentially provide
reprieve

Tremble slowly
the dance rhythm vibrates
mysterious centeredness
subtlety misting grace
celebrating delicacy
two meld into one
beauty in mastery
culmination
revelation

TRUST CHARLES
I have called you friends.
John 15:15

An Attitude of Gratitude

Charles stood up from his walker near the end of the table where he was in the habit of sitting for his meals. His stoutness permitted him to bend just enough from the waist to retrieve his bib from the walker's basket and hand it into thin air in anticipation that one of his friends or caregivers would field the garment. A sympathetic friend carefully took it from his hand. Charles turned a bit and pushed the chair's arm back and away so that he could step into the space between his chair and his place at the table. Without looking, he reached for the chair's arms and sat down heavily with a comfortable sigh, and waited while he caught his breath. His friend waited, too.

The bib was ceremoniously placed as a cloak over his ample paunch and secured by the sound of a snap. Charles shifted his weight more upright and to the back of the chair. Secure and trusting, Charles readied himself for the short push-slide of the chair to the table. His arms had risen with the forward movement of the chair. He placed his arms on the chair's arms and reached for the silverware ready to enjoy steak pie in pastry enhanced with gravy, mashed potatoes, peas, and butternut squash. Charles said, "*Thank you.*" The routine completed, he could relax, tell stories, laugh at some simple joke, and slowly lift the nourishing supper from the plate to his mouth only spilling a little each time as he repeated the ancient ritual of addressing the cuisine before ingesting the meal. For the next three-quarters of an hour Charles enjoyed conversation, laughter, food, and the pleasure of a peaceful meal in a healthy environment.

Charles did not think about trust per se. He knew from experience that a friend, a server, a nurse, or a relative would not tease him in any way to make him anxious. He felt secure. He knew that the people around him would protect him from harm, would care for his needs, and could be trusted to be entirely faithful each and every time to the established form. His meals were free from anxiety. His slow deliberate pace was honoured by those around him by being patient, understanding, and supportive. The food was nutritious. The company was compatible. The expectation was of a carefully orchestrated preparation to dine, to sit, to eat, to finish, and to go about his life as usual in a harmony of people, place, and activity.

Trust is the result of consistent words and deeds on everyone's part. We want to affirm life and the lives of those around us with whom we live and work and worship. We want to affirm that others are valued and appreciated as we would want to be. As community members, we want to create a hospitable environment by recognizing the need to encourage positive attitudes and consistent predictable behaviours free from disrespect, avoidance, or neglect. In short, we want to create a community of trust by our good example.

Trust means that in our relationships, whether at home, places of work, places of recreation, or places of worship, each of us is willing to exhibit positive attitudes, initiate care, and express gratitude to each other. "Think before you speak or act" is proverbial. It is important to ask ourselves, "Is what I am about to say or do, true, helpful, inspiring, necessary, and kind?" Trust is earned.

"*Thank you*," says Charles.

HEALTH
They could not drink the water of Marah because it was bitter.
                                                    Exodus 15:23 *(NRSV)*

Hot, hotter, hottest, humid beyond comfort.
Tropical life knows the rainy season will end.
Rain-break means creek swimming.
Cleansing flood means glops rush away.
"Innocence is bliss."
The thatched village was inconveniently upstream.
Swim above habitation, not below, was the conventional wisdom.
Opportunity beckoned because fast-moving run-off cleansed.
My European wisdom was thrown into the wafting draught.
Walk. Perspire. Check for snakes and effluent.
Shed dhoti, shirt, sandals.
Wade into the water for an alluring bath.
Do not be tempted by the murky water.
Precarious brush, village waste, refuse
hastened atop the swollen stream.
The water's color matched the impoverished soil.
Unwelcome brown sludge wanted to latch.
The filth clung like scum on a boat hull.
Hurried hand-slapping rinsed off offal.
The effect was feeling unsanitary, defiled, filthy
as those with running sores feel unclean.
They did not drink the water because it was bitter.
Inhabitants polluted the stream for centuries
adapting to their pariah status.
Germ theory was unknown, foreign.
Health was a matter of chance.
Health happened. Disease normal. Life expectancy is short.
Stay out of harm's way. Eat simple vegetarian meals.
Drink only boiled water from a "safe" well.
Hot, hotter, hottest, humid, well beyond comfort.
Tropical hope is knowing the rainy season will end.
Preservation follows vital laws.
Salvation requires courageous obedience.

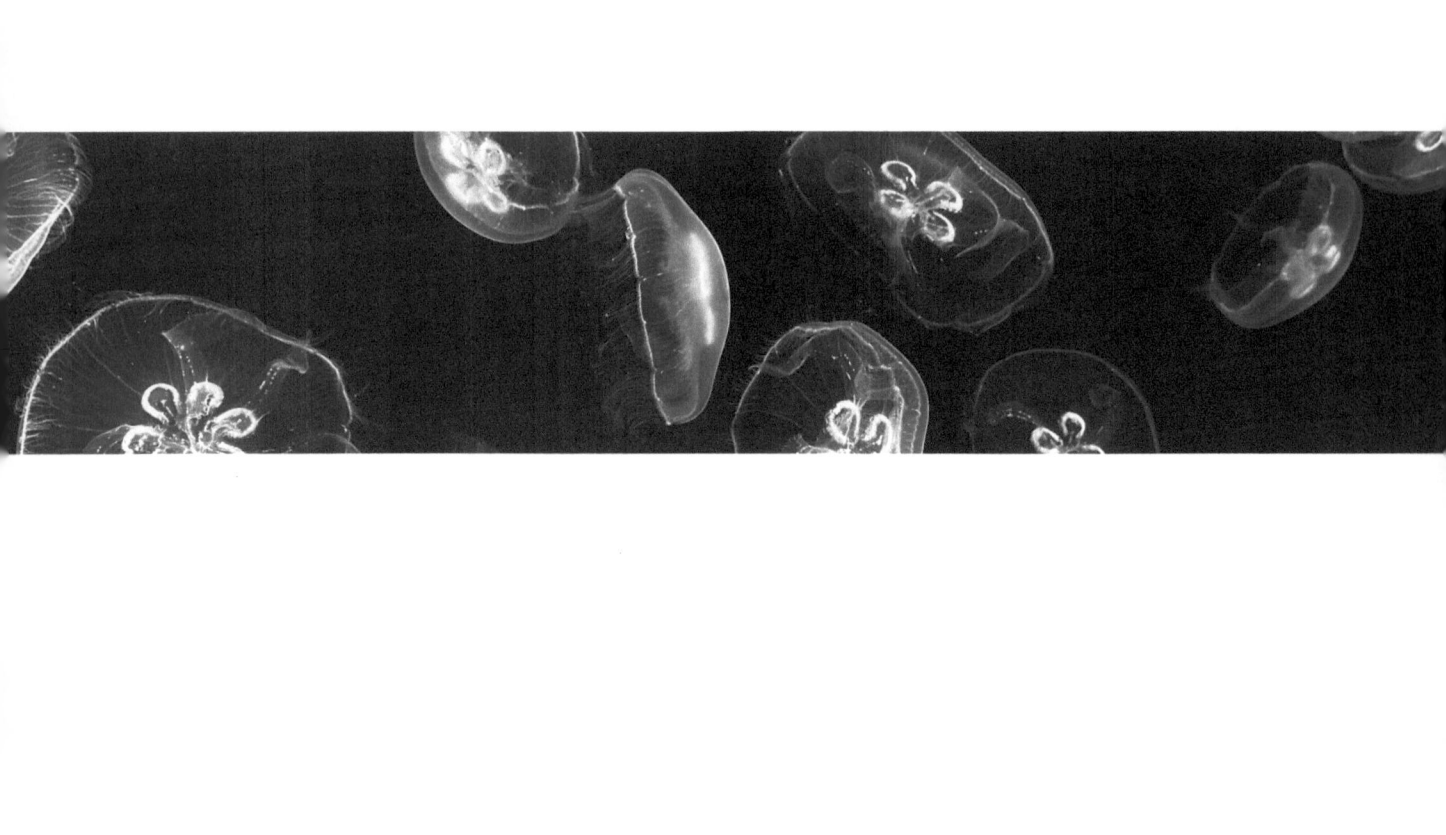

THE QUESTION IS NOT ONE OF MERCY'S GIFTS

*Deep calleth unto deep at the noise of thy waterspouts,
all thy waves and thy billows have gone over me.
Yet, the Lord will command his lovingkindness in the daytime,
and in the night his song shall be with me,
and my prayer unto the God of my life.*

Psalm 42:7-8

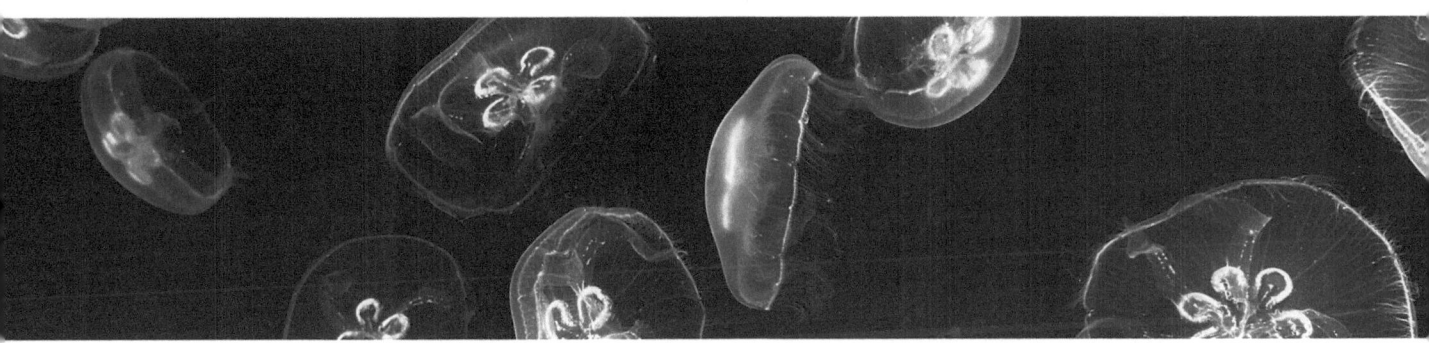

The question is not one of Mercy's gifts.
The question is one of the soul's savors.
In the thrust, the riposte lies in our Lord's favor
In the beauty of life and in the void of a rift
One wants to comply, agree, and strive to deserve
God's tender counter, unmerited forgiveness.

It could be argued that life itself
Challenges and demands one to stop sleeting
Unaware as sheep's narcissistic bleating
Blinded by the tulgey beast of self
One must merge into the Damascus Light
To exculpate that internal ghoulish creature of the night.

Mercy's gift delights in hopeful visions, passionate understandings,
Loving-kindness grants solace to spiritual transformation.

CLOSING PRAYER

Lord our God

You are silently present night and day.
We experience fear, loss, helplessness.
We are blind to desert oases, living waters, thankful hearts.
We are surrounded by beauty, creativity, helping hands.
Your presence is the gift we seek ceaselessly.
       Forgive us when we neglect to pray.

You are our companion, our lifeline of hope, our avatar of love.
We experience loneliness, separation, and failings.
We are blind to connections, friendships, and triumphs.
We are surrounded by dedication, commitment, enterprise, and worthiness.
Your presence is still waiting for us, the calm before the storm.
       Forgive us when we neglect to pray.

You are our inspiration between darkness and revelation.
We experience doubt, chaos, and mystification.
We are blind to confidence, intimacy, and trust.
We are surrounded by skies, fields, streams, mountains, and perilous seas.
Your presence is birth, death, and all matter of things.
       Forgive us when we neglect to pray.

Grant us new eyes, new ears, new hearts, new spirits.
Fill our souls with compassion for all matters of living things.
We humbly kneel, pray, repent, and ask for forgiveness.
       Forgive us when we neglect to pray.

            Amen.

www.ingramcontent.com/pod-product-compliance
Lightning Source LLC
Chambersburg PA
CBHW042248100526
44587CB00002B/64